CELEBRATING THE FAMILY NAME OF ZHU

Celebrating the Family Name of Zhu

Walter the Educator

Silent King Books
a WhichHead Entertainment Imprint

Copyright © 2024 by Walter the Educator

All rights reserved. No part of this book may be reproduced in any manner whatsoever without written permission except in the case of brief quotations embodied in critical articles and reviews.

First Printing, 2024

Disclaimer

This book is a literary work; the story is not about specific persons, locations, situations, and/or circumstances unless mentioned in a historical context. Any resemblance to real persons, locations, situations, and/or circumstances is coincidental. This book is for entertainment and informational purposes only. The author and publisher offer this information without warranties expressed or implied. No matter the grounds, neither the author nor the publisher will be accountable for any losses, injuries, or other damages caused by the reader's use of this book. The use of this book acknowledges an understanding and acceptance of this disclaimer.

Celebrating the Family Name of Zhu is a memory book that belongs to the Celebrating Family Name Book Series by Walter the Educator. Collect them all and more books at WaltertheEducator.com

USE THE EXTRA SPACE TO DOCUMENT YOUR FAMILY MEMORIES THROUGHOUT THE YEARS

ZHU

Zhu, a name of radiant grace,

A timeless thread in history's space.

From ancient courts to skies so blue,

A legacy proud, enduring, true.

Like bamboo standing tall and strong,

The Zhu name echoes in every song.

With roots that delve in earth so deep,

Its wisdom wakes while others sleep.

In whispers soft of scholars' lore,

The Zhu name opens wisdom's door.

A guiding light through storm and tide,

A family bound, side by side.

The crane that soars through skies of gold,

Speaks of Zhu stories brave and bold.

Its wings unfold in beauty rare,

A symbol of honor beyond compare.

Through dynasties' rise, through eras vast,

The Zhu name shines, steadfast, unsurpassed.

A flame of strength, a beacon bright,

It guards the future, claims the night.

In every heart, a spark takes flight,

A Zhu-born dream, a noble sight.

Through fields of toil or city's glow,

The Zhu name thrives, it will not slow.

Like rivers carving paths anew,

The Zhu name flows, steadfast and true.

With every turn, with every bend,

It finds a way, it does not end.

Through crafts and arts, through pens and plows,

The Zhu name rises, making vows.

To honor past, to forge ahead,

With every step, by virtue led.

The Zhu name hums in harmony's song,

A tale of strength where all belong.

With courage vast and hearts sincere,

Its legacy grows year by year.

So here we honor the name of Zhu,

A family noble, strong, and true.

A timeless story, bright and grand,

Forever etched across the land.

ABOUT THE CREATOR

Walter the Educator is one of the pseudonyms for Walter Anderson. Formally educated in Chemistry, Business, and Education, he is an educator, an author, a diverse entrepreneur, and he is the son of a disabled war veteran. "Walter the Educator" shares his time between educating and creating. He holds interests and owns several creative projects that entertain, enlighten, enhance, and educate, hoping to inspire and motivate you. Follow, find new works, and stay up to date with Walter the Educator™

at WaltertheEducator.com

www.ingramcontent.com/pod-product-compliance
Lightning Source LLC
LaVergne TN
LVHW052009060526
838201LV00059B/3936